PUZZLE QUEST
Enchanted lands

written & illustrated
by kia Marie Hunt

Published by Collins
An imprint of HarperCollins Publishers
HarperCollins Publishers
Westerhill Road
Bishopbriggs
Glasgow G64 2QT

www.harpercollins.co.uk

HarperCollins Publishers
1st Floor, Watermarque Building
Ringsend Road
Dublin 4, Ireland

10 9 8 7 6 5 4

ISBN 978-0-00-845746-4

Printed and bound in the UK using 100% renewable electricity
at CPI Group (UK) Ltd

Publisher: Michelle l'Anson
Author and illustrator: Kia Marie Hunt
Project Manager: Sarah Woods
Designer: Kevin Robbins

PUZZLE QUEST

Enchanted lands

written & illustrated
by Kia Marie Hunt

You thought this was just another normal day, until you saw it...

"Saw what??" you ask.

The message in a bottle, of course!

It appeared out of nowhere, just for you.

Inside, you discover a map. Not just any old map – it's a map of:

The Enchanted Lands!

(Get a closer look on the next page)

You're not sure why this map just appeared for you, but you have a sneaky feeling that it's calling you to go on a big adventure!

Follow your map through the Enchanted Lands and be ready to solve more than 100 mysterious and magical puzzles, collecting clues along the way!

Things you'll need:

★ **This book**
★ **A pen or pencil**
★ **Your amazing brain**

That's it!

Will YOU take on the quest?

Psssst!
Always look out for this hand symbol: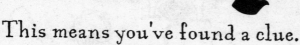

This means you've found a clue.

Write down all the clues you find in your Clue Logbooks (on pages **30**, **54**, **78**, **102** and **128**!)

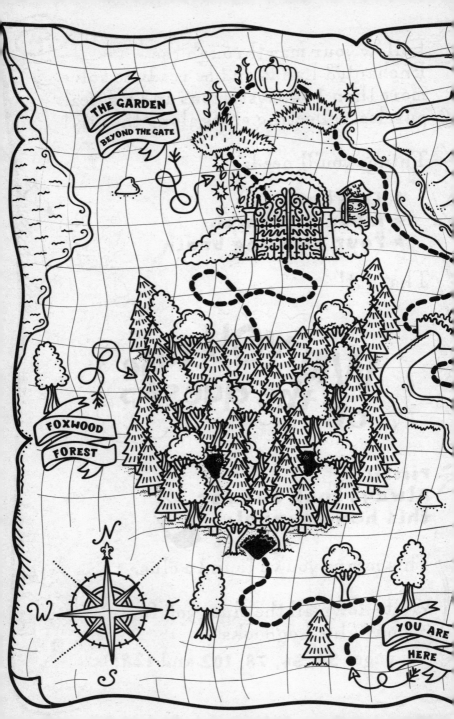

As you step foot into Foxwood Forest, get ready for some woodland word puzzles, nature number games and more forest fun challenges!

You are now entering:

Foxwood Forest

While wandering through the forest, you notice many pairs of glowing eyes watching you from the trees...

Can you spot the five differences between the two spooky pictures above?

Can you make your way through the maze...?

Start

finish!

(Don't let the staring eyes put you off!)

Once you go a little further into the
forest, you realise the eyes just belong
to some very friendly Tree Trolls, phew!
Tree Trolls are named after different kinds
of trees. Can you find all of their names in the
wordsearch on the opposite page?

hello!

Words may be hidden in
the grid horizontally or
vertically.

Watch out! There are eight
Tree Troll names in the list
but only seven can be found
in the wordsearch.
Which is missing?

(This letter is your very
first magical clue,
congratulations! Don't
forget to write it into
your magical clue logbook
on page 30!)

```
        U A G
    E S G J M S L
  T L A L D E R P A
  A Z L A D U H O S T A
  W I L L O W B A B N T
  E L N R S P E V K I A X k
  K M A P L E L N K S Z B W
  T M T X E A A R J G D T T
  Q Y X A B F B A Y E R
  K A S H C R I E L M U
    I V J V Q R A U N
      O U I I C H A
        I M H
```

* OAK
* WILLOW
* ALDER
* MAPLE

* HAZEL
* BIRCH
* ELM
* ASH

The Tree Trolls are so excited to meet you!
They've heard that humans are amazing at
puzzles, so they're curious to know if you
can solve these...

In the sudoku grids below,
the numbers 1, 2, 3 and
4 should be added to each
row, each column and each
2x2 bold outlined box, but
should only appear once in
each one. The first one has
been done for you.

Help the mystical toad hop back across the toadstools to his favourite pond.

You can move up, down or sideways, but you can't move diagonally and you must follow the toadstools in this order:

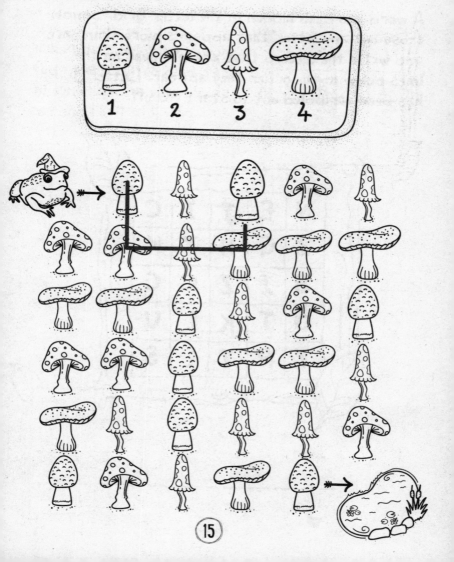

Wow! The Tree Trolls are impressed!
As you're such a great problem-solver, they'd
like your help with a problem they're having.
Can you solve the puzzle below to reveal what
their problem is about?

A word has been hidden in the letter grid. Simply
cross out any letter that appears more than once
and write the letters that are left over on the
lines below in the order they appear. Letter J
has been scribbled out to start you off.

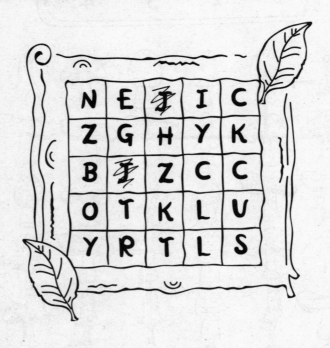

_ _ _ _ _ _ _ _ _ _

These mischievous creatures with long fern leaves growing from their heads are called 'Fern Folk' and they live next door to the Tree Trolls.

The Fern Folk love to play hide and seek. How many of them can you find hiding in the picture below?

So, the Tree Trolls are having some trouble with their neighbours. But it's not the Fern Folk themselves who are the problem, it's their pets – the caterpillars! The caterpillars munch on the Tree Trolls' leaves. Solve the puzzle below to find out why that annoys them so much...

Scribble out every other letter along the caterpillars' bodies to reveal what the problem is. Write the letters that are left over on the lines below. The first two letters on each caterpillar have been done for you.

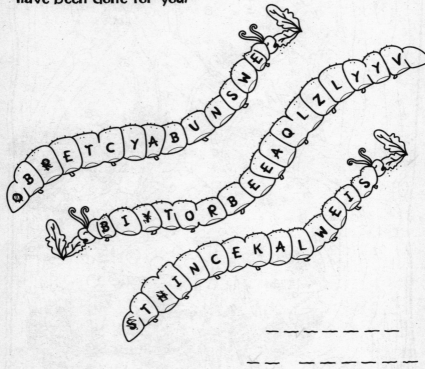

_ _ _ _ _ _ _

_ _ _ _ _ _ _ _

_ _ _ _ _ _ _

Leaves aren't the only thing these caterpillars have been busy chomping on, you can see their nibble marks all over the forest!

Can you match the half-eaten items below to the correct silhouettes? Circle your answers.

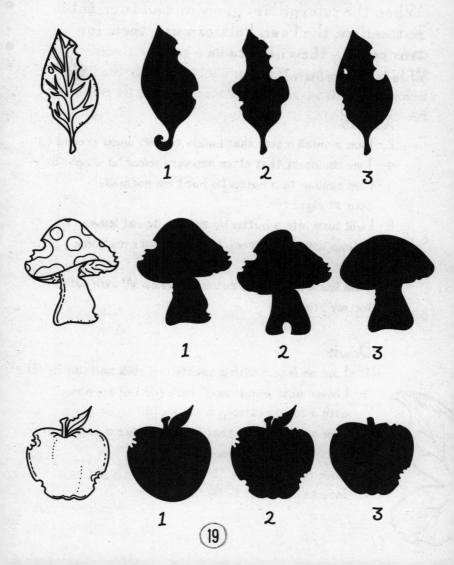

You ask the Fern Folk to set their caterpillar pets free, but it's not that simple!

When the caterpillars grow up and turn into butterflies, the Fern Folk can use them for transport – they need to be able to fly around!

Across
2 - I am a small insect that builds tunnels underground (3) ✓

4 - I am an insect that often has very colourful wings (9) ✓

5 - I am similar to a butterfly but I am normally seen at night (4) ✓

8 - I will turn into a butterfly and like to eat leaves (11) ✓

10 - I jump using my strong legs and share my name with a sport (7) ✓

11 - I am like a bee but do not make honey. Watch out for my sting! (4) ✓

Down
1 - I am an insect with a spotty red shell and can fly (8) ✓

3 - I hover near ponds and share part of my name with a fire-breathing creature (9) ✓

6 - I am a type of bug that looks a lot like a twig (5,6) ✓

7 - This is where honeybees live (4) ✓

9 - I love to make honey (3) ✓

11 - Insects use these to fly (5) ✓

Complete the crossword using the clues on the opposite page.

1 L
2 A N T
3 D
4 B U T T E R F L Y
5 M O T H
6 S
7 H
8 C A T E R P I L L A R
9 B
10 C R I C K E T
11 W A S P

Down words:
LADYBIRD
DRAGONFLY
STICKINSECT
HIVE
BEE
WINGS

Wait a minute... all the Fern Folk you've met have their own wings. So why do they fly around on butterflies? They used to be able to fly, until someone moved their Magic Crystal Cluster. That's when they lost their flying skills and started travelling on butterflies instead.

In the word-wheels, find the names of three other creatures or things that can fly. Each word starts with the centre letter and uses all the letters in the wheel once.

R _ _ _ _ _ _

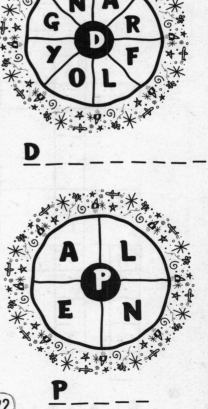

D _ _ _ _ _ _

P _ _ _ _ _

Find your way through the maze, collecting the Magic Crystal Cluster on the way. Then find your way out.

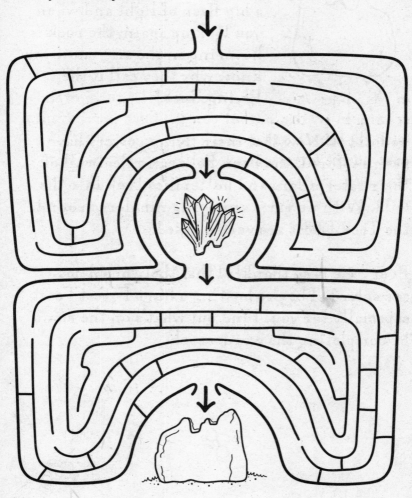

Once the crystal is returned to its rightful place on the Flying Rock, the Fern Folk will be able to fly again!

As soon as you place the Magic Crystal Cluster back into the strange-looking rock, there's a big flash of light and when you look up again, the rock is hovering in the air – now you know why they call it the Flying Rock!

You did it! Now that their flying powers have been restored, the Fern Folk can release all of their caterpillars and butterflies back into the wild. With no more annoying nibblers around, the Tree Trolls are very pleased!

Everyone is so thankful that their problems are solved. They're hosting a huge Forest Feast especially for you! Find out what's on the menu by completing the wordsearch...

There are six tasty treats to look for in the grid, listed below. Cross them off the list when you find them. Words may be hidden in the grid horizontally or vertically.

```
F C H O C O L A T E L O G
L L E A F S Y R U P I P I
M N B V M C R G R G A I Q
B R T T A A U Q R S S N E
W K S R M N D E X L W E L
Y C Y D D D Q I S O I C J
F Q D E R Y R O A R S O O
I U P E T A L P I E U N E
T F D J W C P R C I S E S
W A A E L O D O M F R C I
S K Y B E R R I E S H A K
S R X F E N K S R M Q K T
Y T V G S S L N S J P E K
```

CANDY ACORNS
CHOCOLATE LOG
LEAF SYRUP
PETAL PIE
PINE CONE CAKE
SKY BERRIES

Before you leave, the creatures of Foxwood Forest would like to give you some special gifts!

The Tree Trolls, of course, give you a wooden gift.

Solve the code-cracking puzzle below to find out what it is. Use the grid references to work out each letter. One letter has been done for you.

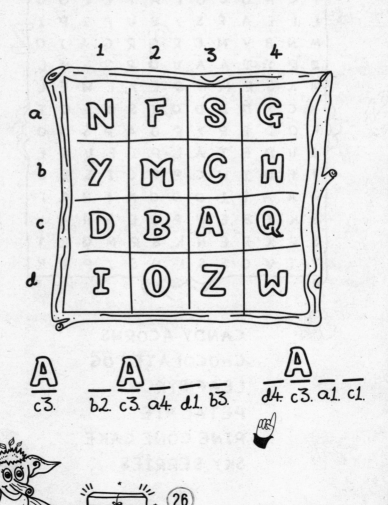

	1	2	3	4
a	N	F	S	G
b	Y	M	C	H
c	D	B	A	Q
d	I	O	Z	W

A
c3.

_ A _ _ _
b2. c3. a4. d1. b3.

_ A _ _
d4. c3. a1. c1.

The Fern Folk give you a box containing
ten very precious leaves...

Can you work out which four letters of the
alphabet are missing above?

Rearrange the missing letters to reveal what
these extraordinary leaves are made of:

__ __ __ __

(Hint: You can scribble out the letters on this alphabet to help you.)

A B C D E F G H I J K L M
N O P Q R S T U V W X Y Z

When leaving Foxwood Forest, you discover three sets of animal footprints...

Can you follow the numbers along each set of footprints and figure out which number is next in the sequence? Write the next number into the circle at the end of the tracks.

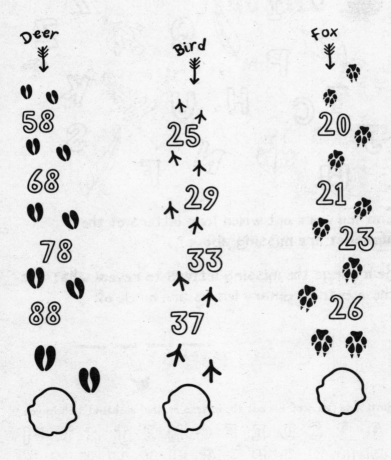

Deer
58
68
78
88

Bird
25
29
33
37

Fox
20
21
23
26

Can you unscramble the letters to form the names of six things you might see while walking along a forest path?

P<u>INECON</u>E = NICENOPE

<u>S</u>QU<u>IRELL</u> = QIRSUREL

<u>M</u>USH<u>ROOM</u> = SOUMHORM

SDIRB TENS = <u>B</u>IRD<u>S</u> N<u>EST</u>

<u>S</u>IGNPOS<u>T</u> = GINSTOPS

ETER MUPST = <u>T</u>R<u>EE</u> S<u>TUMP</u>

(Look closely, there are clues hidden everywhere!)

Clue Logbook: Foxwood Forest

Before you continue on your adventure, use this logbook to record any clues you found in Foxwood Forest.

Remember, clues are pointed out by this symbol: 👉

Write the clue letter next to the page number you found it on!

Page: 12   Clue letter: [ ]

Page: 16   Clue letter: [ ]

Page: 21   Clue letter: [ ]

Page: 26   Clue letter: [ ]

Page: 27   Clue letter: [ ]

You are now leaving
Foxwood Forest
Thanks for visiting!

(Blank 'notes' pages like this
are handy for jotting down
any notes or working-out
when you're busy solving
puzzles! There are some extra
note pages at the back too.)

Go through the gate and get ready to discover pumpkin patches, potions and puzzles. Take care though, there are rumours that a witch lives past these gates, hidden somewhere among the magical gardens...

(Clue Logbook for this chapter is on Page 54!)

THE GARDEN BEYOND THE GATE...

As you get closer, you notice lots of keys growing from the enchanted hedges next to the gates. Each key is different...

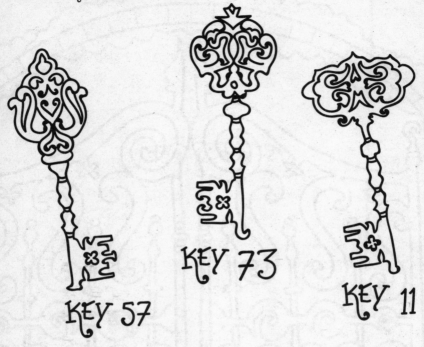

KEY 57

KEY 73

KEY 11

By looking at the silhouette inside the padlock, can you figure out which is the correct key to unlock the gates?

Write your answer here: Key __ __

You may have the right key for the padlock but you also need to say the magic word 'PARSNIP' before the gates will finally open for you.

Can you find the complete word in the bubble below?

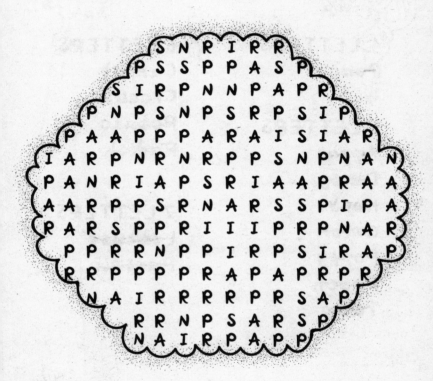

Inside the gates, you discover a lush garden brimming with life.

Place each of the words, from the lists below, into the empty squares to create a filled crossword grid. Each word is used once so cross it off as you place it to help you keep track.

4 LETTERS
Pear

5 LETTERS
Apple
Daisy
Herbs
Onion
Poppy
Peach
Tulip

6 LETTERS
Carrot
Crocus
Potato
Radish

7 LETTERS
Lettuce
Parsnip

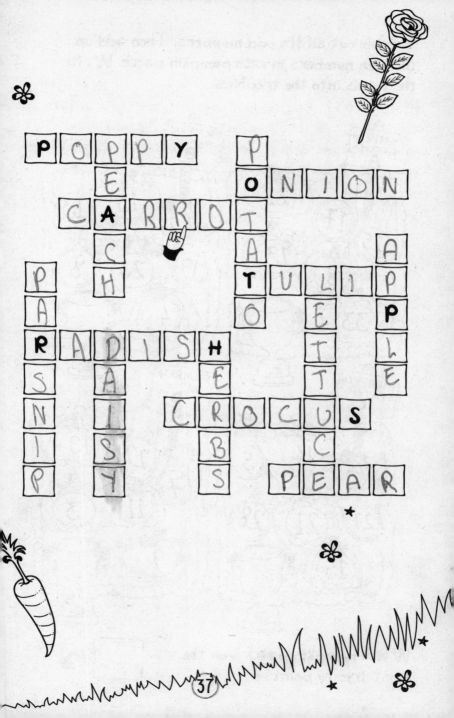

POPPY · P
PEACH · ONION
CARROT · POTATO
PEACH
PARSNIP · RADISH · APPLE
PARSNIP · TULIP
RADISH · HERBS · LETTUCE
DAISY · CROCUS · PEAR

Sribble out all the odd numbers. Then add up the even numbers in each pumpkin patch. Write the totals into the trophies.

Which pumpkin patch won the most trophy points?

What's that you see at the centre of the
pumpkin patches? It's a very curious cottage!

Can you make your way through the maze
to get there?

It's quite dark inside the cottage, but you can see plenty of signs that the rumours are true: a witch really does live here!

M S R C F D Q Q Q N K P
Q B Z M M I A C T R L C
N O R D L U A C S E B R
T P C X Q M N P O T Z U
W A X D W Z E I N N Q A
I S C A N L L I B A T S
B B N K L B K O I L K L
D D R B C P O T I O N H
N H O O M A T O K G C E
C O Q U O N L R N Y Y R
K Q P D A M M B Z I S B
R Y E J M J O N L P A S

Can you find nine witchy items in the wordsearch from the list below? Watch out! One of them is missing. Words may be hidden in the grid horizontally, vertically, diagonally or backwards.

POTION   CAULDRON
BROOM   BLACK CAT
WAND   LANTERN
HERBS   PUMPKIN
CANDLE   SPELL BOOK

Which witchy item is missing from the wordsearch?

— — — — — — — — ☝

If a witch does live here, should you be scared...?

Suddenly, a movement catches your eye.
There's something lurking behind the door...

A dark and spooky
silhouette moves
towards you.

Feeling brave, you
open the door...

One witch doesn't live here, two do! Thankfully neither of them look as scary as you thought they would!

Let's get to know the Witch Twins. Solve the puzzles to find out their names...

Scribble out every other letter. To reveal the name of the smiling witch, write the letters that are left over on the lines below. The first letter has been scribbled out for you.

H _ _ _ _ _ _

To reveal the name of the shy witch hiding behind her twin, use the grid references to work out each letter. Two letters have been done for you.

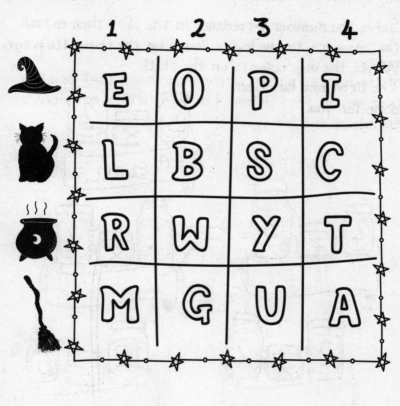

	1	2	3	4
🎩	E	O	P	I
🐱	L	B	S	C
🖤	R	W	Y	T
🧹	M	G	U	A

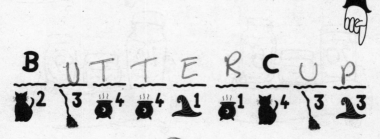

B U T T E R C U P
🐱2 🧹3 🖤4 🖤4 🎩1 🖤1 🐱4 🧹3 🎩3

43

The shelves below are where the Twins store their weird and wonderful potion ingredients. But their jars don't have labels, and getting ingredients mixed up could be disastrous!

Solve the number problems in the jars then match the answers to the ingredients on the opposite page. Write the ingredients on the shelf. The first one has been done for you.

$5 \times 2 =$ eyeballs

$4 + 5$

1×2

2×2

$12 - 6$

$20 - 6$

$10 + 9$

(You can tick the box next to each ingredient once it has been labelled and stored on the shelf!)

10 eyeballs ✓

4 eggshells ☐

14 crystal dust ☐

5 unicorn horns ☐

2 nettles ☐

19 dragon scales ☐

9 spiders ☐

6 feathers ☐

Which of the ingredients above isn't on any of the shelves?

_____

There are four cauldrons bubbling: three contain something yummy, one contains something dangerous. The problem is, the Twins have forgotten which cauldron is which!

Unscramble the letters in each cauldron to reveal what's brewing inside them.

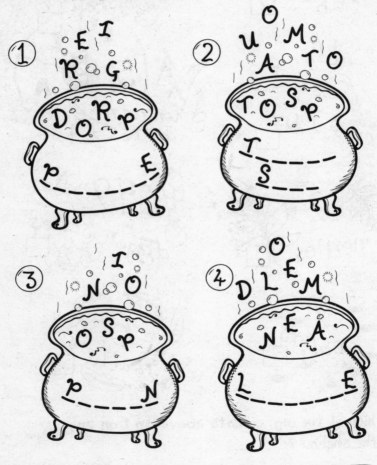

Which of the four cauldrons contains the dangerous liquid?

Rearrange the letters in the three word-wheels to form the names of potion ingredients. Start with the centre letter and use all the letters in the wheel once.

(Hint: all of these ingredients are insects.)

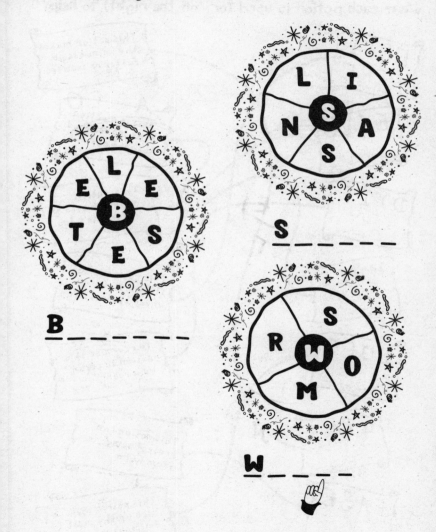

B _ _ _ _ _ _

S _ _ _ _ _

W _ _ _ _

Some pages have fallen out of the witches' potion recipe book!

Unscramble the letters on the left to reveal the potion names. These are linked to an explanation of what each potion is used for (on the right) to help.

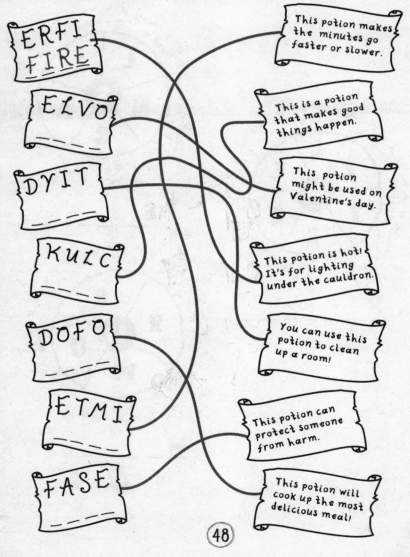

ERFI FIRE
_ _ _ _ _ _ _ _

ELVO
_ _ _ _

DYIT
_ _ _ _

KULC
_ _ _ _

DOFO
_ _ _ _

ETMI
_ _ _ _

FASE
_ _ _ _

This potion makes the minutes go faster or slower.

This is a potion that makes good things happen.

This potion might be used on Valentine's day.

This potion is hot! It's for lighting under the cauldron.

You can use this potion to clean up a room!

This potion can protect someone from harm.

This potion will cook up the most delicious meal!

Making a witch's brew is always a complicated task! Before you can add the teabag to the teacup, you have to get through this strange collection of teapots.

You can move up, down or sideways, but you can't move diagonally and you must follow the teapots in this order:

1   2   3   4

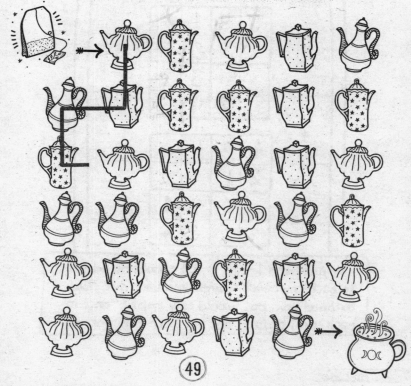

You've helped the Witch Twins with their potions, but can you help them solve their biggest problem?

Solve the sudoku puzzles so you can take a look through the enchanted window.

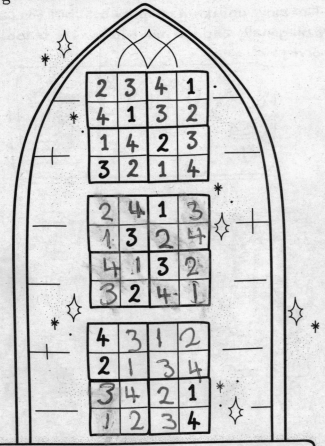

The numbers 1, 2, 3 and 4 should be added to each row, each column and each 2x2 bold outlined box, but should only appear once in each one. The first one has been done for you.

Look through the enchanted window to see into the future. Is something bad about to happen?

Shade in or scribble out all the squares containing the letters B, K, W and Y. The remaining letters will spell out what you discover from the vision in the window.

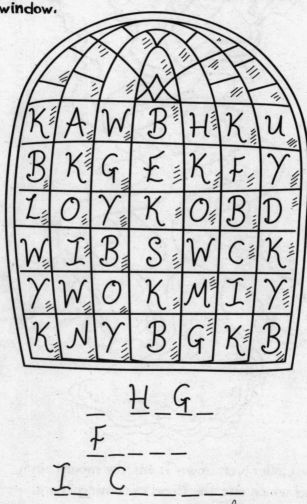

_ H _ G _

F _ _ _ _

I _ C _ _ _ _ _

Oh no! This vision of the future is bad news. A huge flood would ruin the Witch Twins' magical gardens!

Follow each river down from the mountains, to find which one the flood is coming from. Write your answer in the box.

It's time for you to leave Pumpkin Cottage...

Find the path that takes you from Pumpkin Cottage to the river. You must visit each magic garden only once on the way. Use one line to connect each garden. Whatever you do, don't travel along the same path twice!

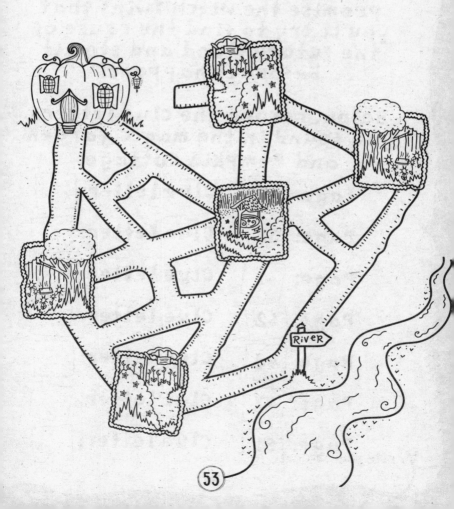

Clue Logbook: The Garden beyond the Gate

It's now time to continue your adventure. Before you go, you promise the Witch Twins that you'll try to find the cause of the future flood and stop it before it happens!

Below, record the clue letters you found in the magic garden and Pumpkin Cottage.

Page: 37   Clue letter: ☐

Page: 38   Clue letter: ☐

Page: 41   Clue letter: ☐

Page: 42   Clue letter: ☐

Page: 43   Clue letter: ☐

Page: 47   Clue letter: ☐

Page: 51   Clue letter: ☐

Notes:

This way to the Great Lake
Follow the river all the way to the Great Lake...
As well as plenty of watery word puzzles and flooded fun number games, you might be surprised by what else you will find there!

(Clue Logbook for this chapter is on Page 78!)

Place each of the words into the empty squares to create a filled crossword grid. Each word is used once so cross it off as you place it to help you keep track.

4 LETTERS
Carp
Fish

5 LETTERS
Canoe
Ducks
Frogs
Heron
Otter
Reeds
Stoat
Trout

6 LETTERS
Minnow

7 LETTERS
Insects

9 LETTERS
Dragonfly
Water vole

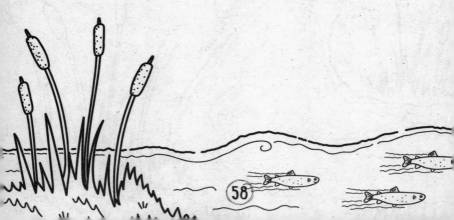

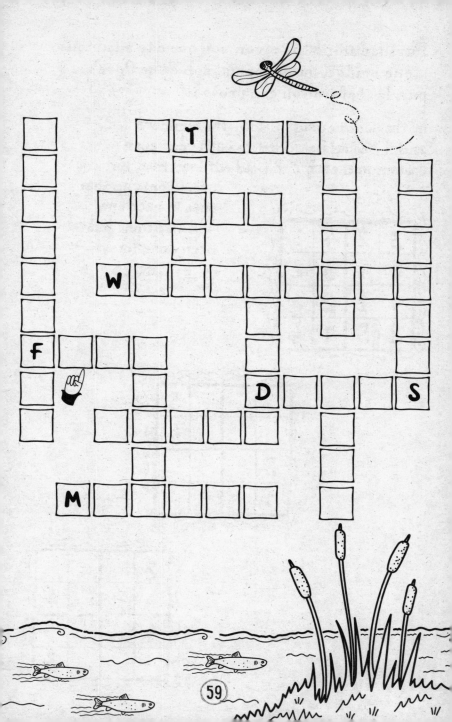

Further along the river, you come to a curious stone bridge, but you must solve the Ogre's puzzles before you can cross it!

In the sudoku grids below, the numbers 1, 2, 3 and 4 should be added to each row, each column and each 2x2 bold outlined box, but should only appear once in each one. The first one has been done for you.

3	2	4	1
1	4	3	2
4	1	2	3
2	3	1	4

			3
			4
3			
1			

2			
			4
4			
			3

Solve the number problem below each letter in the Key.
Then use the answers to fill in the Ogre's message.
The first one has been done for you.

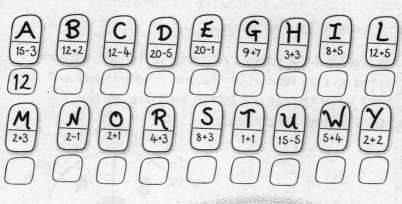

A	B	C	D	E	G	H	I	L
15-3	12+2	12-4	20-5	20-1	9+7	3+3	8+5	12+5
12								

M	N	O	R	S	T	U	W	Y
2+3	2-1	2+1	4+3	8+3	1+1	15-5	5+4	2+2

$$\overline{}_{4} \ \overline{}_{3} \ \overline{}_{10} \quad \overline{}_{5} \ \overline{A}_{12} \ \overline{}_{4} \quad \overline{}_{1} \ \overline{}_{3} \ \overline{}_{9}$$

$$\overline{}_{8} \ \overline{}_{7} \ \overline{}_{3} \ \overline{}_{11} \ \overline{}_{11} \quad \overline{}_{2} \ \overline{}_{6} \ \overline{}_{19} \quad \overline{}_{14} \ \overline{}_{7} \ \overline{}_{13} \ \overline{}_{15} \ \overline{}_{16} \ \overline{}_{19} \ ,$$

$$\overline{}_{9} \ \overline{}_{19} \ \overline{}_{17} \ \overline{}_{17} \quad \overline{}_{15} \ \overline{}_{3} \ \overline{}_{1} \ \overline{}_{19} \ !$$

61

The Ogre used to live under the bridge but the water has risen so high that there's no space left under there any more! All of the water in the area is starting to overflow and no one knows why...

Can you find the names of three different water-themed words hidden in the word-wheels below? Start with the centre letter and use all the letters in the wheel once.

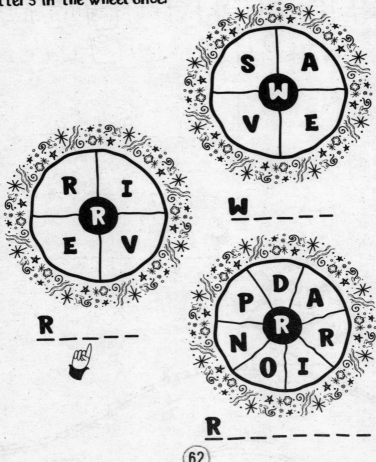

S A W E V

W _ _ _ _

R I R E V

R _ _ _ _ _

P D A R R N O I

R _ _ _ _ _ _ _

Hop across the flooded stream from start to finish.

You can move up, down or sideways, but you can't move diagonally and you must follow the stepping stones in this order:

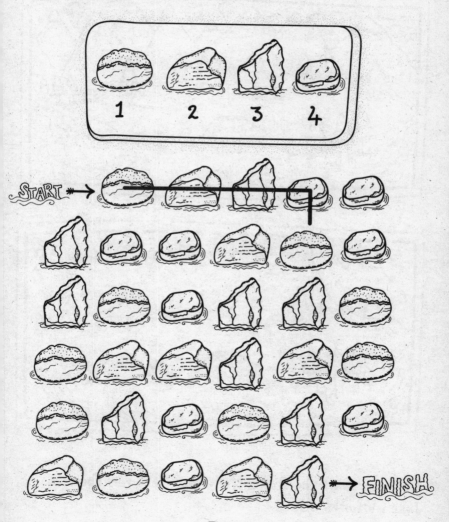

At the foot of the mountains, you discover a huge lake. Just like the Ogre said, it's overflowing! This must be where the big flood begins...

Can you spot the five differences between the two lake pictures above?

This lake is full of strange-looking islands...

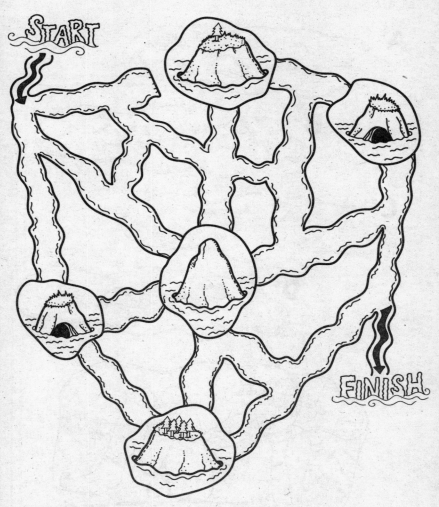

Use the watery paths to make your way from start to finish. You must visit each island only once on the way. Use one straight line to connect each island. Whatever you do, don't travel along the same path twice!

Wait a minute... some of these aren't islands at all!

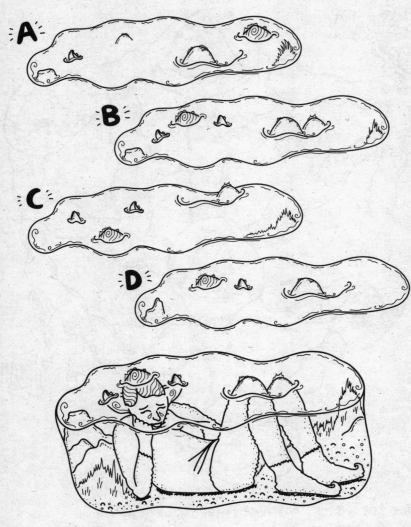

A

B

C

D

Which group of 'islands' matches the shape of the sulky Giant hiding at the bottom of the lake?

Aha! So that's where all of the water is coming from – this poor Giant has been crying and their enormous tears are causing everything to overflow!

Which lagoon is the deepest? Scribble out any even numbers, then add up all of the odd numbers in each lagoon and write the totals into the circles! The lagoon with the highest total is the deepest.

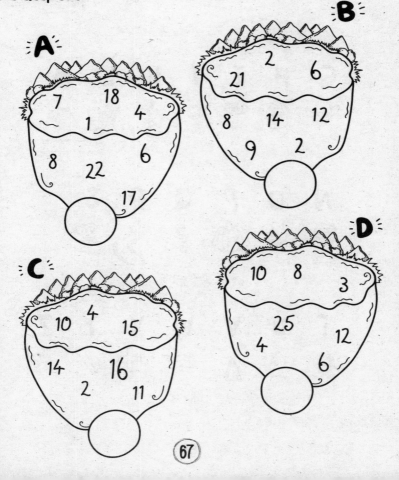

The Giant seems very upset... perhaps you can cheer them up!

Use the symbol key to crack the codes and reveal the punchlines to some funny jokes. Maybe they'll make the Giant laugh.

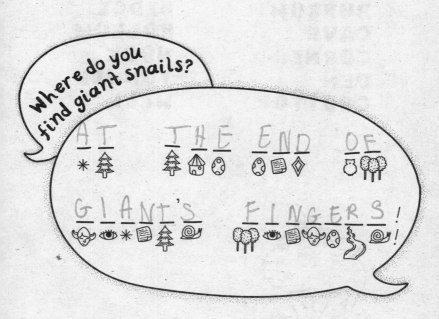

69

Even your jokes couldn't cheer up the Giant! That's because the Giant's best friend, Piggy, has gone missing! Can you help find her?

You search high and low for the missing Piggy. Where can she be?

Find the hiding places in the grid on the opposite page and cross each one off the list when you find it. Words may be hidden in the grid horizontally or vertically.
Watch out! One of them is missing...

BURROW
CAVE
CORNER
DEN
GROTTO

HEDGE
HOLLOW
NOOK
TUNNEL
WELL

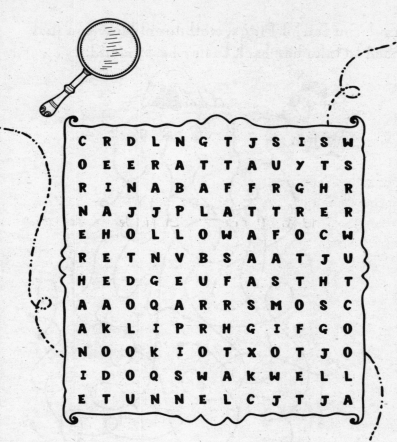

```
C R D L N G T J S I S W
O E E R A T T A U Y T S
R I N A B A F F R G H R
N A J J P L A T T R E R
E H O L L O W A F O C W
R E T N V B S A A T J U
H E D G E U F A S T H T
A A O Q A R R S M O S C
A K L I P R H G I F G O
N O O K I O T X O T J O
I D O Q S W A K W E L L
E T U N N E L C J T J A
```

There are ten hiding places in the list but only nine of them can be found in the wordsearch.
Which hiding place is missing?

_____

(That's where you'll find Piggy!)

Yay! You found Piggy, well done! Now you just need to take her back to her best friend...

Which of the tangled paths leads back to the Giant at the lake? Write your answer in the box.

Now they're happily reunited, the Giant (who has finally stopped crying!) has a poem for you...

Follow the lines and write the letter from each circle in the space at the end of each line to reveal a new word.

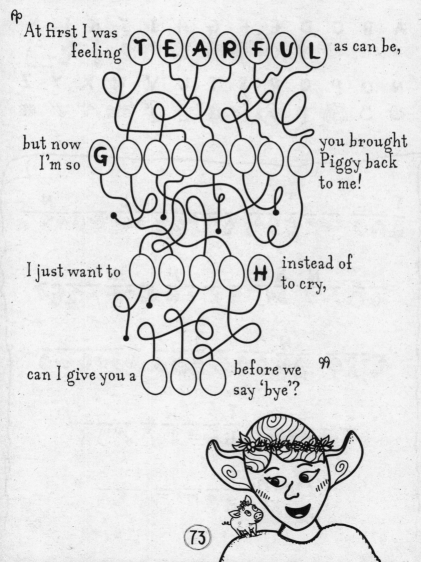

At first I was feeling **TEARFUL** as can be,

but now I'm so **G**◯◯◯◯◯◯ you brought Piggy back to me!

I just want to ◯◯◯◯**H** instead of to cry,

can I give you a ◯◯◯ before we say 'bye'?

What's that flying over? It looks like a
raven, and it has some letters for you!

Crack the codes using the Key below to
reveal what's inside each message...

A B C D E F G H I J K L M

N O P Q R S T U V W X Y Z

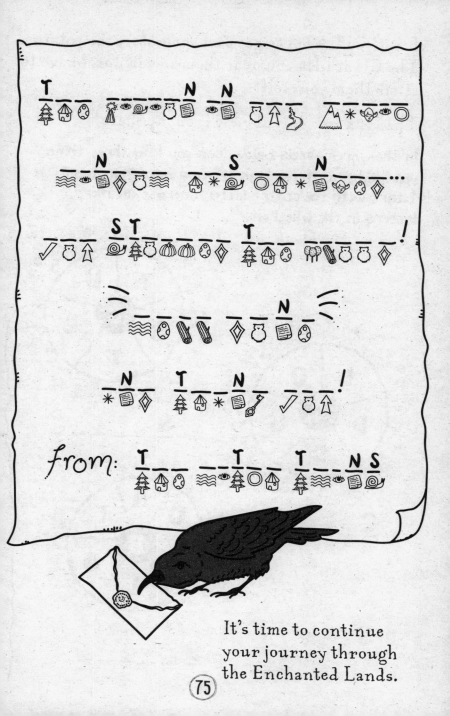

from:

It's time to continue
your journey through
the Enchanted Lands.

First you'll need to get past some steep mountains. The Giant lifts you over them so you don't have to climb them yourself!

There's a wonderful view from up there!

In the word-wheels below, can you find three things you might see from high above a mountain top? Start with the centre letter and use all the letters in the wheel once.

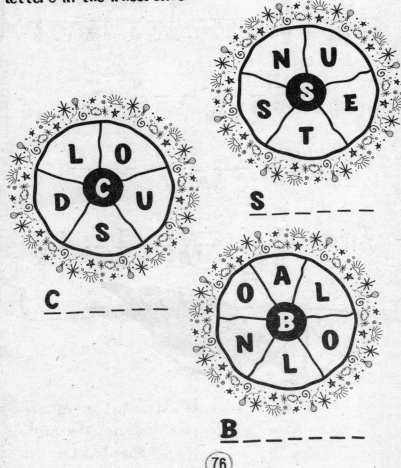

C _ _ _ _ _ _

S _ _ _ _ _ _

B _ _ _ _ _ _

From the other side of the mountains, can you find which path will lead you to Sandshell Bay?
Write your answer in the box.

Clue Logbook: The Great Lake

It's time to continue your adventure through the Enchanted Lands. Now that the Giant has lifted you over the mountains, you can make your way to Sandshell Bay...

Below, record any clue letters you found near the Great Lake.

Page: 59   Clue letter:

Page: 61   Clue letter:

Page: 62   Clue letter:

Page: 66   Clue letter:

Page: 72   Clue letter:

Notes:

.(Clue Logbook for this chapter is on Page 102)

Welcome to SANDSHELL BAY

When you get to the bay, it's completely dry. How strange...

Where has the sea gone?

You might just find the answer if you take on the beachy brain-teasers and coastal conundrums in this sandy chapter of your adventure.

Make your way through the maze, across the dry bay, to reach the shells you can see in the distance...

Let's collect some seashells!
You can move up, down or sideways, but you can't move diagonally and you must follow the shells in this order:

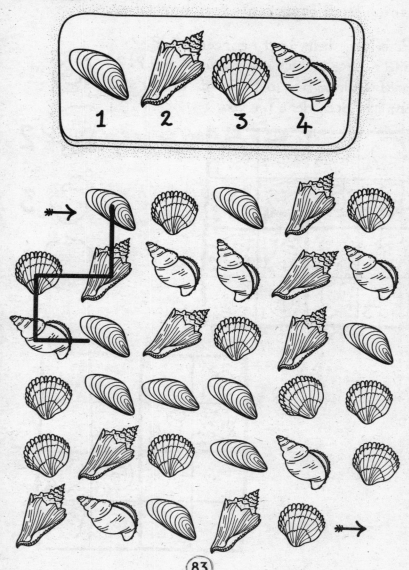

Each shell in the sudoku puzzles below is equal to a number from 1 to 4.

To begin, first look at the key below to see which shell represents which number.

Place the shells that represent 1, 2, 3 and 4 once in each row, column and 2x2 bold outlined box in the grid. The first one has been done for you.

Can you find which of the silhouettes matches the large shell below?

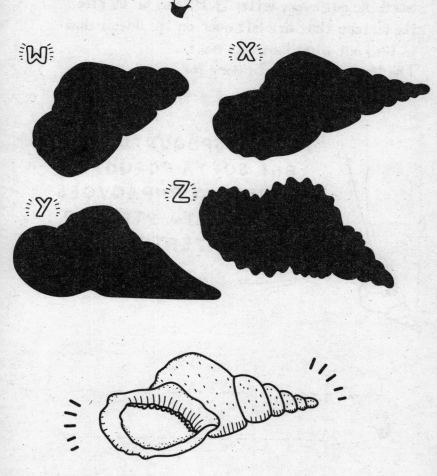

This feels like a very special shell, it's heavy and when you put it to your ear, you can hear the sounds of the sea!

Why not try using the shell like a horn? Blow into it to make a VERY LOUD sound, then solve the puzzle below to find out what happens!

Scribble out every letter J, P, and Q. Write the letters that are left over on the lines below to find out what happens next...
The first one has been done for you.

JTPHQE SPOQUNJDP OQF
TPHE SQEJA PGRQOJWS.
PGQRJEAJT PWPAQVQES
RJOPLL QIJN. PTQHJEP
JSPEQA RJEPTQUJRNPS!

T__ ____ __ __ ____ ____...

____ ____ ___ __...

___ ___ _____!

Looking closely at the waves, you notice lots of peculiar little faces beginning to appear...

How many Shell Elves can you count in the image above?

(Don't be fooled by all the other shells they're hiding amongst!)

This calls for a celebration. Help the Shell
Elves prepare a cake for their Sea Festival by
completing the puzzle...

Solve the number problem on each cake layer
then match the answer to the icing flavour on
the opposite page. Write the flavour next to
the cake layer. The first one has been done
for you.

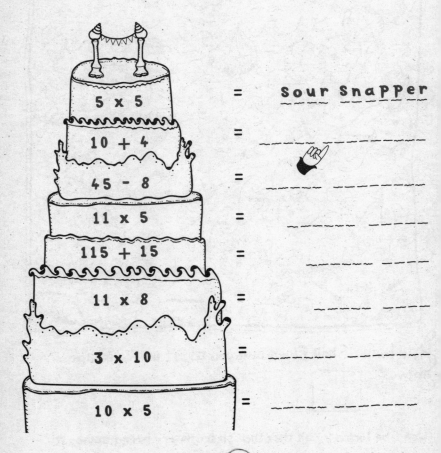

5 x 5   =   <u>Sour Snapper</u>

10 + 4   =   _ _ _ _ _ _ _ _ _ _

45 - 8   =   _ _ _ _ _ _ _ _ _ _

11 x 5   =   _ _ _ _ _ _ _ _ _ _

115 + 15   =   _ _ _ _ _ _ _ _ _ _

11 x 8   =   _ _ _ _ _ _ _ _ _ _

3 x 10   =   _ _ _ _ _ _ _ _ _ _

10 x 5   =   _ _ _ _ _ _ _ _ _ _

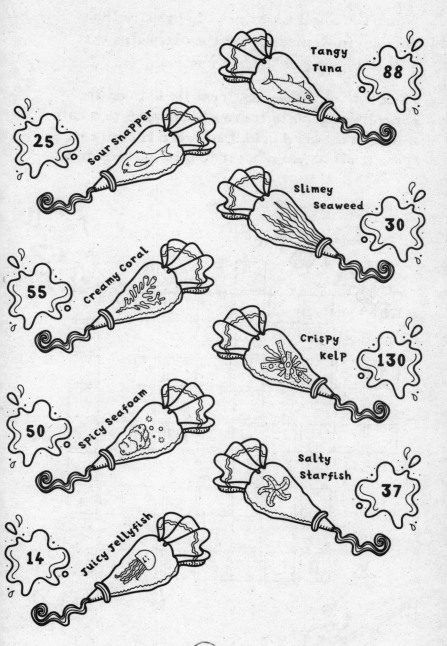

Tangy Tuna 88

Sour Snapper 25

Slimey Seaweed 30

Creamy Coral 55

Crispy Kelp 130

Spicy Seafoam 50

Salty Starfish 37

Juicy Jellyfish 14

Next, the Shell Elves need to prepare the musical instruments for the orchestra that will be playing at the Sea Festival...

Place each of the words, from the lists on the opposite page, into the empty squares to create a filled crossword grid. Each word is used once so cross it off as you place it to help you keep track.

4 LETTERS
Harp

5 LETTERS
Flute

6 LETTERS
Violin

7 LETTERS
Bassoon
Trumpet

8 LETTERS
Clarinet
Trombone

10 LETTERS
Double bass

There's just one problem... the Star Musician of the whole orchestra (who can play eight instruments at once) has gone missing!

You must help the Shell Elves find the Musician before the evening of the Sea Festival...

Can you find all of the places where you search for the Musician in the wordsearch?

Find each of the places (see list on opposite page) in the grid and cross it off the list when you find it. Words may be hidden in the grid horizontally or vertically.

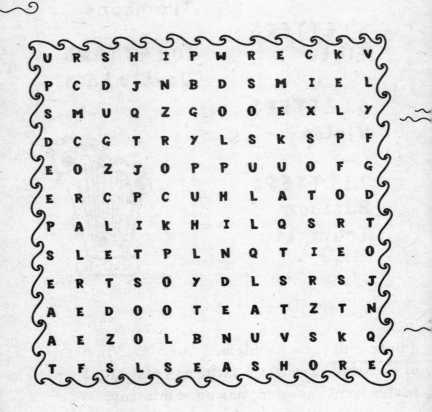

```
U R S H I P W R E C K V
P C D J N B D S M I E L
S M U Q Z G O O E X L Y
D C G T R Y L S K S P F
E O Z J O P P U U O F G
E R C P C U H L A T O D
P A L I K H I L Q S R T
S L E T P L N Q T I E O
E R T S O Y D L S R S J
A E D O O T E A T Z T N
A E Z O L B N U V S K Q
T F S L S E A S H O R E
```

CORAL REEF   **ROCK POOLS**

DEEP SEA   **SEASHORE**

DOLPHIN DEN   **SHIPWRECK**

KELP FOREST

There's one other place you haven't looked...

Follow the lines and write the letter from each circle in the space at the end of each line to find out where you should search next.

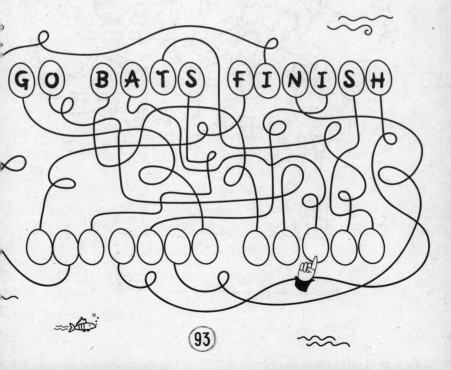

Oh no! You find the Musician, but they're all tangled up in a fishing net!

Scribble out every other letter. Write the letters that are left over on the lines below to reveal what the Musician is saying to you. The first letter has been done for you.

H _ _ _   _ _
_ _ _ _ _ _ !

You need to pull on one of these four ropes to set the Musician free.

Pull on the correct rope to set the Musician free!

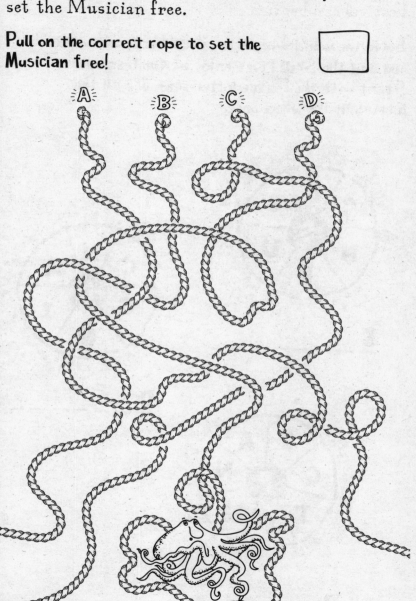

Yay! Now you've rescued the Musician, the Sea Festival can begin!

Solve the word-wheels to reveal three activities you and the Shell Elves enjoy at the festival. Start with the centre letter and use all the letters in the wheel once.

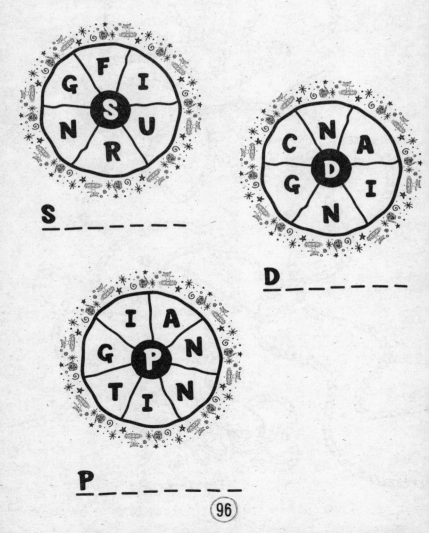

S _ _ _ _ _ _

D _ _ _ _ _ _

P _ _ _ _ _ _

One of the Shell Elves has a riddle for you.

"I may have a face, but I am not a person.
I may control the waves, but I live in the sky.
I may be seen at night, but I am not a star.
I may be full, but I never eat.
What am I?"

Use the code-cracker puzzle below to solve the riddle.
Did you get the answer right?

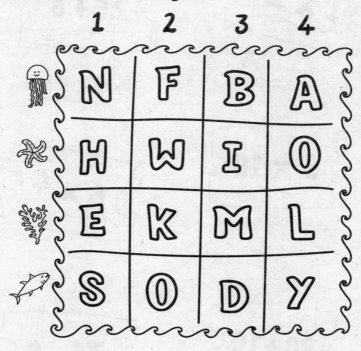

3. 2. 4. 1.

The Shell Elves are having a Sea Festival raffle!

Help them find out which prizes they got by solving the number problem on each raffle ticket, then matching the answers to the prizes on the opposite page. The first one has been done for you.

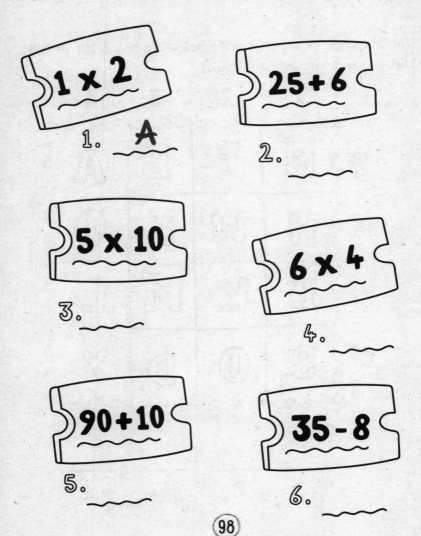

1 x 2

1. **A**

25 + 6

2. ___

5 x 10

3. ___

6 x 4

4. ___

90 + 10

5. ___

35 - 8

6. ___

Prize A!
2

Prize B!
24

Prize C!
27

Prize D!
31
SeaTV

Prize E!
50

Prize F!
100

You can't get to where you're going next because a volcano is in the way! Luckily, the Shell Elves know of a secret tunnel you can use...

Can you make your way down through the maze, to the centre, then come up on the other side?

start

finish

Follow the lines and write the letter from each circle into the space at the end of each line to reveal two volcano-themed words...

Clue Logbook: Sandshell Bay

As you make your way through the Shell Elves' secret tunnel under the volcano, you wonder what you will discover on the other side, in the final part of your Enchanted Lands adventure...

Below, record any clue letters you found at Sandshell Bay.

Page: 85   Clue letter:

Page: 86   Clue letter:

Page: 88   Clue letter:

Page: 90   Clue letter:

Page: 93   Clue letter:

Notes:

MAKING MAGIC!

On the other side of the tunnel, you find yourself at the start of a long, winding path that leads all the way up to the building in the sky...

That's the Magic Academy, which means your adventure through the Enchanted Lands is almost complete! Can you solve the magic mind games in this chapter?

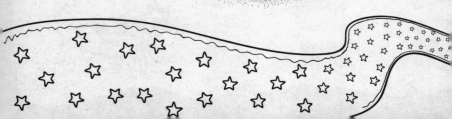

(Clue Logbook for this chapter is on Page 128!)

Phew! That was a long walk but you finally made it up the path and through the clouds. Welcome to the Magic Academy!

Can you spot the seven differences between these two pictures of the Magic Academy?

This is where young witches, wizards and
other magic folk come from all over the
Enchanted Lands to study their craft and do
marvellous things...

First, you try to enter the Magic Academy through one of the doorways...

Use the code-cracker below to reveal a message from the door.

	1	2	3	4
◎	O	K	E	N
⚑	R	S	A	B
◍	P	Q	L	Y
☽	V	W	H	G

G __ __   A __ __ __ !
☽4. ◎1.   ⚑3. ☽2. ⚑3. ◍4.

How rude! Well, if you can't get in through the doorway, maybe you'll have better luck through the window...

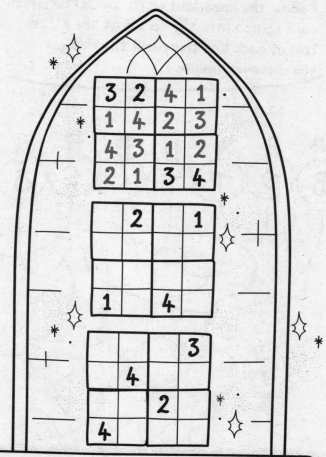

The numbers 1, 2, 3 and 4 should be added to each row, each column and each bold outlined box, but should only appear once in each one. The first one has been done for you.

You find yourself in a Wizard's study.

Follow the lines and write the letter from each object into the space at the other end of each line to reveal the things you discover inside.

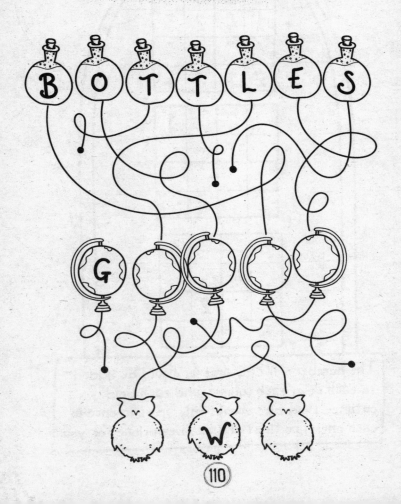

Look through each telescope and connect the stars by following the numbers. Reveal the message that the Wizard has left for you, written in the stars!

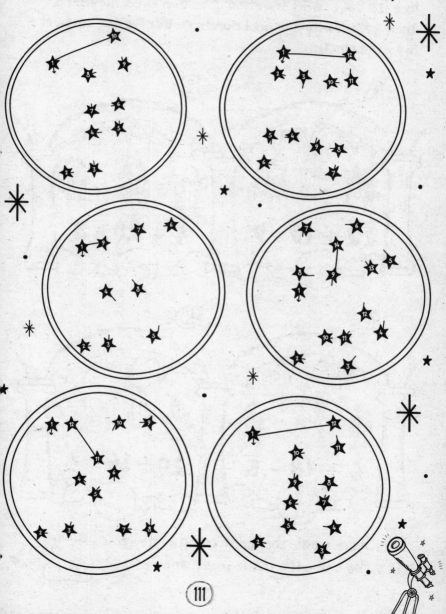

First, you look for the Wizard in the basement, which is full of incredible crystal caves!

In each cave, add together the two even numbers then take away the odd number. Write the answers into the circles.

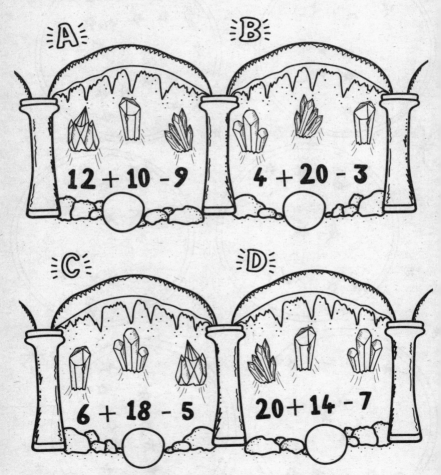

A: 12 + 10 - 9

B: 4 + 20 - 3

C: 6 + 18 - 5

D: 20 + 14 - 7

Which cave has the most crystal power? (It's the one with the highest answer.)

To get to the other side of the basement, you can move up, down or sideways, but you can't move diagonally and you must follow the crystals in this order:

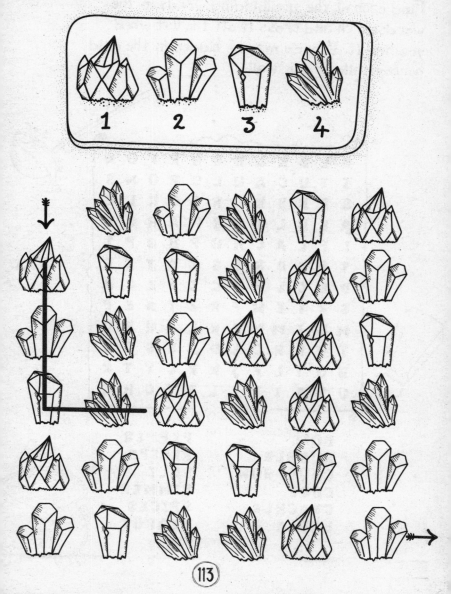

Next, you search the Magic Academy's kitchen, which is brimming with wonderful sights, sounds and smells!

Find each of the spellbinding words in the wordsearch and cross it off the list when you find it. Words may be hidden in the grid horizontally or vertically.

A	L	B	K	L	R	S	U	P	T	O	A
I	I	U	C	A	U	L	D	R	O	N	S
S	P	B	S	K	C	R	A	C	K	L	E
A	E	B	L	T	R	S	H	A	R	S	R
L	P	L	A	C	H	O	P	B	B	P	T
T	P	E	D	S	T	S	Z	A	J	I	E
D	E	C	L	R	E	C	I	P	E	C	A
S	R	T	E	W	P	R	Z	T	A	E	P
M	S	I	M	M	E	R	L	L	O	S	O
T	R	F	R	C	L	D	J	S	S	O	T
B	O	I	L	F	J	K	R	C	T	I	K
U	T	A	I	P	L	L	A	I	C	H	Q

BOIL
BUBBLE
CAULDRON
CHOP
CRACKLE
LADLE

PEPPER
RECIPE
SALT
SIMMER
SPICES
TEAPOT

What's on the Magic Academy menu this week?

Solve the number problem below each letter in the Key. Then use the answers to fill in the menu. The first one has been done for you.

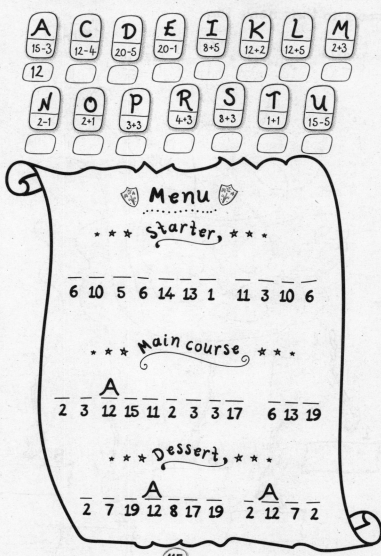

A	C	D	E	I	K	L	M
15-3	12-4	20-5	20-1	8+5	12+2	12+5	2+3
12							

N	O	P	R	S	T	U
2-1	2+1	3+3	4+3	8+3	1+1	15-5

🛡 Menu 🛡

* * * Starter * * *

__ __ __ __ __ __ __ __ __ __ __
6 10 5 6 14 13 1 11 3 10 6

* * * Main course * * *

__ __ A̲ __ __ __ __ __ __ __ __ __
2 3 12 15 11 2 3 3 17 6 13 19

* * * Dessert * * *

__ __ A̲ __ __ __ __ __ A̲ __ __
2 7 19 12 8 17 19 2 12 7 2

You try looking for the Wizard in the cupboard under the stairs, but loads of magic brooms come flying out!

Follow the lines to match each **Wizard** or **Witch's** broom to their name tag.

Can you match the magical tools and objects below to the correct silhouettes? Circle the correct answer.

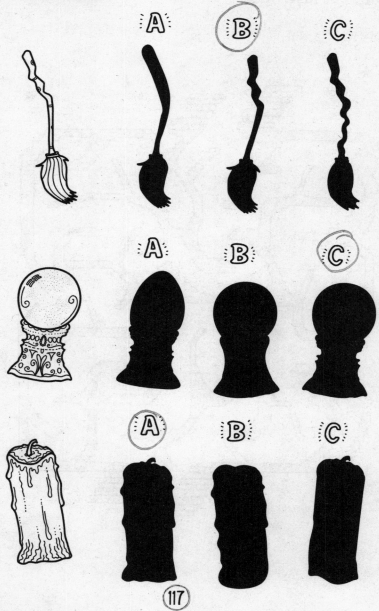

Let's look for the Wizard upstairs. Can you make your way through the maze of staircases? Don't get lost!

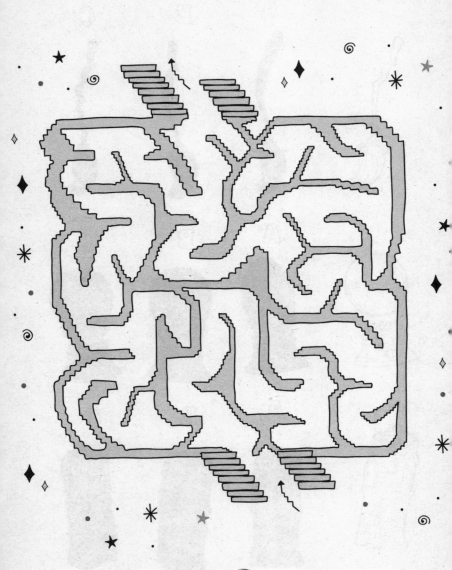

Can you follow the numbers along each set of stairs and figure out which number is next in the sequence? Write the next number into the star at the top of the stairs.

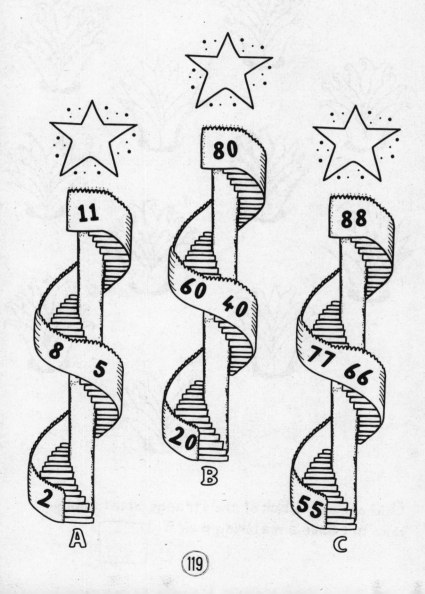

Up on the roof, you search a rather enchanted greenhouse...

Odd one out: which of the strange plants above does not have a matching pair?

Scribble out every other letter. Write the letters that are left over on the lines below to reveal a message the Wizard has left for you. The first letter has been done for you.

G E G T J T K I N N V G E C D L R O S S O E P R B

G _ _ _ _ _ _ _   _ _ _ _ _
GETTING CLOSER

Getting closer? Let's keep looking!

Through a little trap door, you find yourself in the Magic Academy's Pet Pen.

Follow the lines and write the letter from each circle into the space at the other end of the line to discover some of the weird and wonderful animals that assist the Witches and Wizards in their magic.

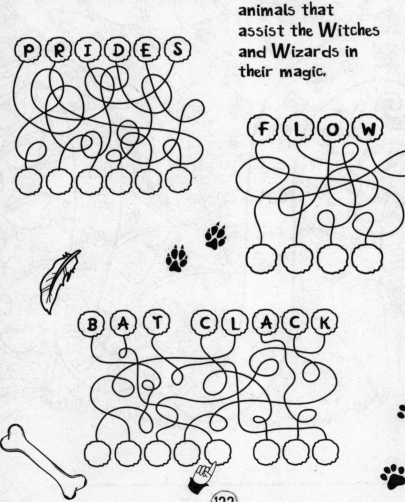

P R I D E S

F L O W

B A T   C L A C K

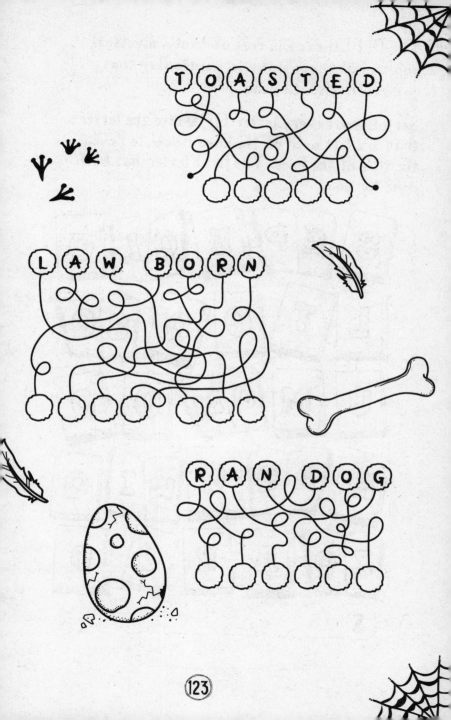

The Old Library is full of dusty, mystical books, but there's one in particular that you really should read...

Scribble out every letter Q. Write the letters that are left over on the lines below to reveal the title of the book. The first letter has been done for you.

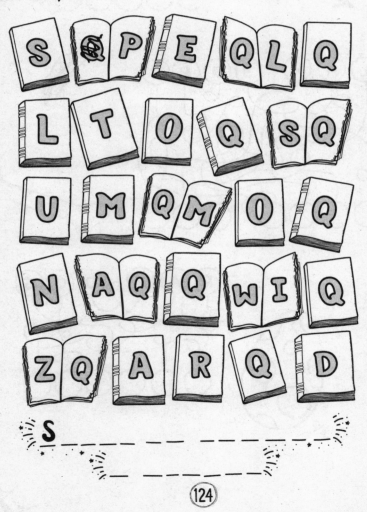

S _ _ _ _   _ _   _ _ _ _ _ _   _   _ _ _ _ _ _

Inside the book, you find a list of spell ingredients.

Use the symbol key below to crack the code and discover which ingredients you need. Some letters have already been done for you.

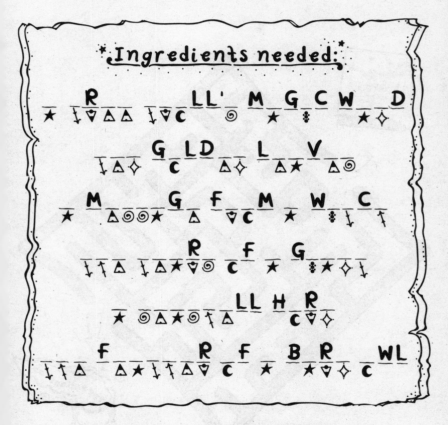

·Ingredients needed:·

_R_ _ _ _ _   _ _LL'_ _M_G_C_W_ _D
★ ↓▽△△ ↓▽C   ◎ ★ ⁙ ★◇

_G_LD   _L_   _V_
↓△◇ C △◇ △★ △◎

_M_ _ _G_F_M_W_C_
★ △◎◎★ △ ▽C ★ ⁙↓ ↓

_ _ _ _R_ _ _F_ _G_
↓↑△ ↓△★▽◎ C ★ ⁙★◇↓

_ _ _ _ _ _LL H R
★ ◎△★◎↓△   C▽◇

_ _ _ _ _R_F_BR_WL
↓↑△ △★↓↑△▽C ★ ★▽◇C

A E H I N O R S T
★ △ ↑ ⁙ ◇ C ♡ ◎ ↓

It looks like you already have all the ingredients for this spell. It's time to take them to the Potions Lab and see what you can do.

Can you make it through the maze from the Library to the Lab?

In the Lab, you find six bottles. Only one of them has the magic powers you'll need for your big spell!

Follow the tangled lines to find which bottle is labelled 'Magic'. Write your answer in the box.

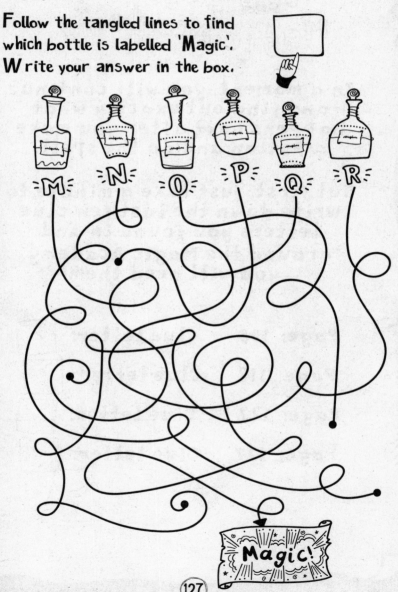

M   N   O   P   Q   R

Magic!

Clue Logbook: Magic Academy

In a moment, you will continue and find out exactly what happens next after you make a potion and do the spell.

But first, just take a minute to write down the last few clue letters you found in and around the Magic Academy – you will need them!

Page: 108   Clue letter: [ ]

Page: 112   Clue letter: [ ]

Page: 122   Clue letter: [ ]

Page: 127   Clue letter: [ ]

Using the magic potion bottle and
all the ingredients you collected
from your Enchanted Lands quest,
you make a strange purple potion.

With your new potion, you follow
the instructions you found in the
Old Spell Book.

Crack the code on the next pages
to reveal the end of the story...

Crack the Code to finish the story!

Look back at all five Clue Logbooks on Pages 30, 54, 78, 102 and 128. Write the clue letters into the key below:

(For example, because you found the letter 'Z' on Page 12, the letter 'Z' is in the '12' box)

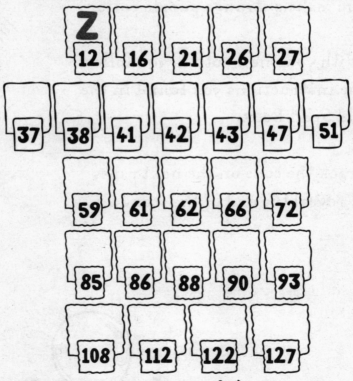

Z				
12	16	21	26	27

37	38	41	42	43	47	51

59	61	62	66	72

85	86	88	90	93

108	112	122	127

Once your key is complete, you can crack the code to reveal the story ending!

POOF! IN A BIG CLOUD OF PURPLE
SMOKE, THE _ _ _ _ _ _ APPEARS!
26 59 12 93 37 112

" _ _ _ _ _ _ _ _ !
16 59 38 41   26 90 37 122

"YOU COMPLETED THE SPELL TO
S _ _ _ _ _ ME, AND YOU ALSO
61 42 47 47 90 16

_ _ _ _ _ _ THE TEST."
43 93 61 61 41 112

? ?   "WHAT TEST?" YOU ASK.   ? ?
? ?   ?
? ?   THE W _ _ _ _ _   L _ _ _ _ _ ...   ?
?   26 59 12 93 37 112 27 93 42 51 86 61   ? ?

"WHO DO YOU THINK SENT THAT
M _ _ IN A _ _ _ _ _ _ TO YOU?"
47 93 43   66 90 21 21 27 41

IT WAS THE W _ _ _ _ _ WHO SENT
26 59 12 93 37 112

YOU ON A _ _ _ _ _ TO TEST YOU.
127 42 41 61 21

YOU ARE NOW _ _ _ _ _ _ _
59 16 62 59 21 41 112

TO _ _ _ _ THE
88 90 59 16

_ _ _ _ _ _ _ _ _ _ _ _ !
47 93 51 59 38 93 38 93 112 41 47 108

(131)

Congratulations

on completing your quest!
The adventure isn't over
just yet...

You'll find more Puzzle Quest
fun online at
collins.co.uk/puzzlequest

But wait!

You'll need the secret password...

Use the key from page 130 to crack
the code and reveal your answer!

The secret password is

$\overline{26}$ $\overline{59}$ $\overline{12}$ $\overline{93}$ $\overline{37}$ $\overline{112}$

PUZZLE
Answers

Page 10 – Spot the Difference

Page 14 – Sudoku

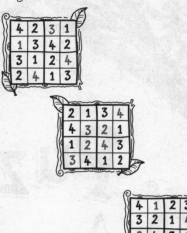

Page 11 – Maze

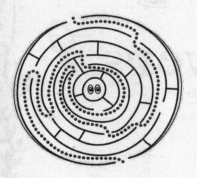

Pages 12 & 13 – Wordsearch

Page 15 – Toadstool Game

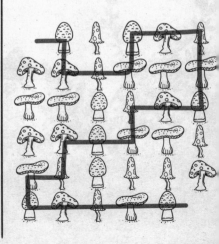

Page 16 – Wordfinder Puzzle

NEIGHBOURS

Page 17 – Hide and Seek

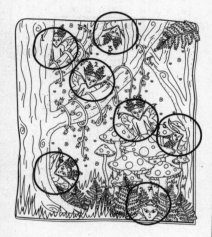

There are seven
Fern Folk hiding

Page 18 – Word Scribble

BECAUSE
IT REALLY
TICKLES

Page 19 – Silhouette Match

③ /

① /

② /

Pages 20 & 21 – Crossword

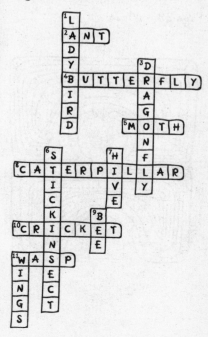

Page 22 – Word-Wheels

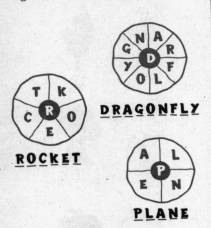

ROCKET

DRAGONFLY

PLANE

Page 25 – Wordsearch

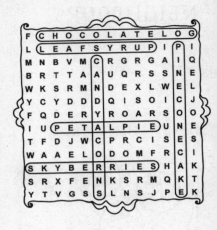

Page 26 – Code Puzzle

A MAGIC WAND

Page 27 – Missing Letters

GOLD

Page 23 – Maze

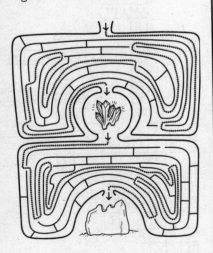

Page 28 – Footprint Sequence

Deer	Bird	Fox
98	41	30

Page 29 – Word Scramble

PINECONE
SQUIRREL
MUSHROOM
BIRDS NEST
SIGNPOST
TREE STUMP

Page 34 – Key Code

11

Page 35 – Wordfinder

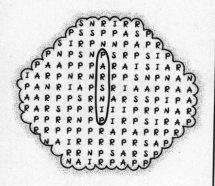

Pages 36 & 37 – Kriss Kross

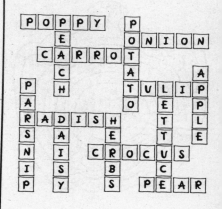

Page 38 – Maths Game

C won the most
trophy points.

Page 39 – Maze

Page 40 – Wordsearch

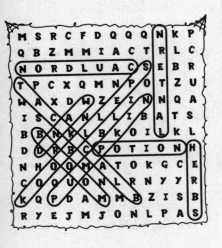

Page 41 – Missing word

CANDLE

Page 42 – Word Scribble

HUBBARD

Page 43 – Code Puzzle

BUTTERCUP

Pages 44 & 45 –
Ingredients Game

SPIDERS (4+5=9)
NETTLES (1x2=2)
EGGSHELLS
(2x2=4)
FEATHERS (12-6=6)
CRYSTAL DUST
   (20-6=14)
DRAGON SCALES
(10+9=19)

Page 45 – Potion Ingredients

5
UNICORN HORNS

Page 46 – Word Scramble

1 PORRIDGE
2 TOMATO SOUP
3 POISON
4 LEMONADE

Cauldron 3 contains the
dangerous liquid

Page 47 – Word-Wheels

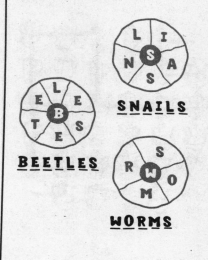

SNAILS

BEETLES

WORMS

Page 48 – Potion Names

ERFI
FIRE

ELVO
LOVE

DYIT
TIDY

KUZC
LUCK

DOFO
FOOD

ETMI
TIME

FASE
SAFE

Page 49 – Teapot Game

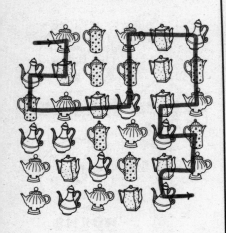

Page 50 – Sudoku

2	3	4	1
4	1	3	2
1	4	2	3
3	2	1	4

2	4	1	3
1	3	2	4
4	1	3	2
3	2	4	1

4	3	1	2
2	1	4	3
3	4	2	1
1	2	3	4

Page 51 – Wordfinder Puzzle

A HUGE
FLOOD
IS COMING

Page 52 – Flood Puzzle

Page 53 – Maze

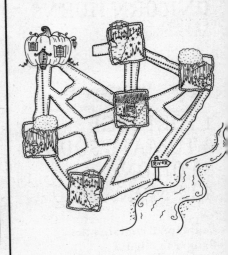

Pages 58 & 59 – Kriss Kross

```
D     O T T E R       C           I
R     R           S T O A T   A   N
A     U               U       N   S
G     W A T E R V O L E       E   E
O     E               E   E       C
F I S H               E   E       T
L     E               D U C K S   S
Y   F R O G S             A
    O                     R
  M I N N O W             P
```

Page 60 – Sudoku

```
3 2 4 1
1 4 3 2
4 1 2 3
2 3 1 4
```

```
4 1 2 3
2 3 1 4
3 2 4 1
1 4 3 2
```

```
2 4 3 1
3 1 2 4
4 3 1 2
1 2 4 3
```

Page 61 – Ogre Maths

YOU MAY NOW CROSS THE BRIDGE, WELL DONE!

A – 12   M – 5
B – 14   N – 1
C – 8   O – 3
D – 15   R – 7
E – 19   S – 11
G – 16   T – 2
H – 6   U – 10
I – 13   W – 9
L – 17   Y – 4

Page 62 – Word-Wheels

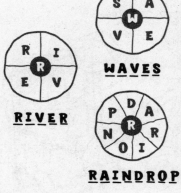

RIVER

WAVES

RAINDROP

Page 63 – Stepping Stones

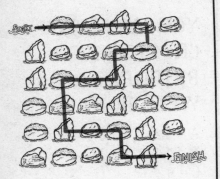

Page 64 – Spot the Difference

Page 65 – Maze

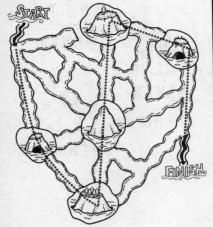

Page 66 – Island Match

Page 67 – Lagoon Maths

A 25
B 30
C 26
D 28

The deepest lagoon is B

Page 69 – Code-Cracker 1

YOU USE
BIG WORDS!

AT THE END OF GIANT'S FINGERS!

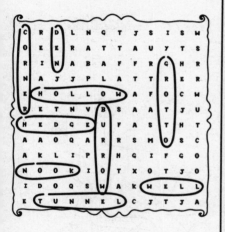

Piggy is hiding in the cave

TEARFUL GRATEFUL LAUGH HUG

Page 74 – Code-Cracker

THE WATER
LEVEL IS GOING
DOWN SO I CAN
FINALLY LIVE
UNDER THE BRIDGE
AGAIN. THANK YOU!
FROM: THE OGRE

Page 75 – Code-Cracker

THE VISION IN OUR
MAGIC WINDOW
HAS CHANGED...
YOU STOPPED THE
FLOOD!
WELL DONE AND
THANK YOU!
FROM: THE WITCH
TWINS

Page 76 – Word-Wheels

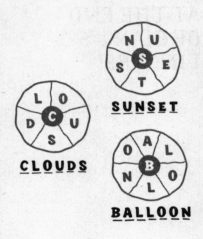

SUNSET

CLOUDS

BALLOON

Page 77 – Tangled Paths

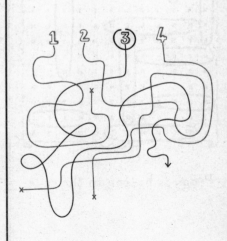

Page 82 - Maze

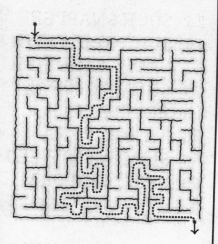

Page 83 - Seashell Game

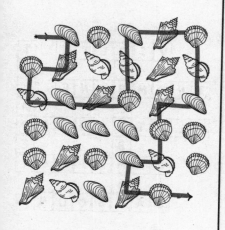

Page 84 - Seashell Sudoku

Page 85 - Seashell Silhouette

Page 86 – Letter Game

THE SOUND OF THE
SEA GROWS...
GREAT WAVES
ROLL IN...
THE SEA RETURNS!

Page 87 – Hide and Seek

There are 11 Shell Elves

Page 88 – Icing Game

25 SOUR SNAPPER
14 JUICY JELLYFISH
37 SALTY STARFISH
55 CREAMY CORAL
130 CRISPY KELP
88 TANGY TUNA
30 SLIMEY SEAWEED
50 SPICY SEAFOAM

Pages 90 & 91 – Kriss Kross

```
          D
  V I O L I N        T
          U          R
T R O M B O N E      U
          L          M
F L U T E B   H A R P E
          A          T
  C L A R I N E T
          S
  B A S S O O N
```

Page 92 – Wordsearch

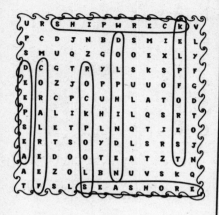

Page 94 – Word Scribble

HELP ME
PLEASE !

Page 93 – Word Tangle

FISHING BOATS

Page 95 – Tangled Ropes

Page 96 – Word-Wheels

SURFING

DANCING

PAINTING

Pages 98 & 99 – Raffle Maths

1 A
2 D
3 E
4 B
5 F
6 C

Page 100 – Maze

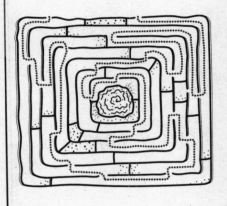

Page 97 – Code Puzzle

MOON

Page 101 – Word Tangle

CRATER

ERUPTS

Pages 106 & 107 – Spot the Difference

Page 108 – Code Puzzle

GO AWAY!

Page 109 – Sudoku

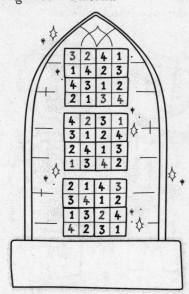

Page 110 – Word Tangle

BOTTLES
GLOBE
OWL

Page 111 –
Telescope Join the Stars

FIND ME

Page 112 – Crystal Maths Game

A   13
B   21
C   19
D   27

The cave with the most
crystal power is D

Page 113 – Crystal Game

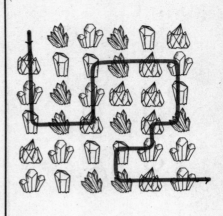

Page 114 – Wordsearch

Page 115 – Menu Puzzle

PUMPKIN SOUP
TOADSTOOL PIE
TREACLE TART

A – 12   N – 1
C – 8   O – 3
D – 15   P – 6
E – 19   R – 7
I – 13   S – 11
K – 14   T – 2
L – 17   U – 10
M – 5

Page 116 – Broom Tangle

1 Sabrina
2 Merlin
3 Winnie
4 Harry
5 Mildred

Page 117 – Silhouette Match

Page 118 – Maze

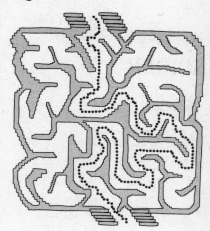

Page 119 – Staircase Sequence

A	B	C
14	100	99

Page 120 – Odd One Out

Page 121 – Word Sribble

GETTING CLOSER

Page 122 – Word Tangle

SPIDER

WOLF

BLACK CAT

Page 123 – Word Tangle

TOADS

BARN OWL

DRAGON

Page 124 – Letter Game

SPELL TO
SUMMON
A WIZARD

Page 125 – Code-Cracker

A TREE TROLL'S
MAGIC WAND

TEN GOLDEN LEAVES

A MESSAGE FROM A
WITCH

THE TEARS OF A
GIANT

A SEASHELL HORN

THE FEATHER OF A
BARN OWL

Page 126 – Maze

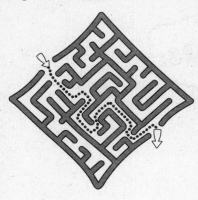

Page 127 – Tangled Lines

Page 130 – Clue Code

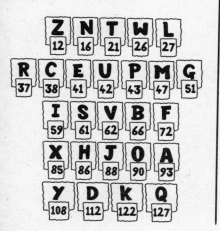

Pages 130 & 131 –
Code-Cracker

POOF! IN A BIG CLOUD
OF PURPLE SMOKE,
THE WIZARD
APPEARS!

NICE WORK!

"YOU COMPLETED THE
SPELL TO SUMMON
ME AND YOU ALSO
PASSED THE TEST."

"WHAT TEST?" YOU
ASK. THE WIZARD
LAUGHS...

"WHO DO YOU THINK
SENT THAT MAP IN A
BOTTLE TO YOU?"
IT WAS THE WIZARD
WHO SENT YOU ON A
QUEST TO TEST YOU.

YOU ARE NOW
INVITED TO JOIN THE
MAGIC ACADEMY!

(Blank 'notes' pages like this are handy for jotting down any notes or working-out when you're busy solving puzzles! You could also use them to write, doodle, or anything else you'd like to do while on your adventure through the Enchanted Lands!)

Notes:

Notes: